Write On...
RAINFORESTS

Clare Hibbert

W

FRANKLIN WATTS
LONDON•SYDNEY

Franklin Watts
First published in Great Britain in 2016 by The Watts Publishing Group

Credits
Series Editor: Melanie Palmer
Conceived and produced by Hollow Pond
Editor: Clare Hibbert @ Hollow Pond
Designer: Amy McSimpson @ Hollow Pond
Illustrations: Kate Sheppard
Photographs: Alamy: 5 (Steve Bloom Images), 6–7 (Joe Austin Photography),
9 (imageBROKER), 12–13 (Andy Selinger), 15 (Arco Images GmbH), 17
(PhotoAlto), 18–19 (Danita Delimont), 25 (Eddie Gerald), 26–27 (Sue
Cunningham Photographic); Shutterstock: cover (Dirk Ercken), 10–11
(Don Mammoser), 21 (Pierre-Yves Babelon), 22–23 (Amy Nichole Harris),
29 (jointstar, rook76, Dirk Ercken, cybervelvet). Every attempt has been
made to clear copyright. Should there be any inadvertent omission please
apply to the publisher for rectification.

ISBN 978 1 4451 5011 6

Printed in China

FSC
www.fsc.org
MIX
Paper from
responsible sources
FSC® C104740

Franklin Watts
An imprint of
Hachette Children's Group
Part of The Watts Publishing Group
Carmelite House
50 Victoria Embankment
London EC4Y 0DZ

An Hachette UK Company
www.hachette.co.uk

www.franklinwatts.co.uk

You can help to save
rainforests. Raise some
money and donate it
to an organisation such
as Rainforest Alliance
(their website address
is on page 31).

Look out for the **Write On...** writing tips and tools
scattered through the book, then head to the Writing school on
page 28 for project ideas to inspire your awesome inner author.

Please return/renew this item by the last date above. You can renew on-line at
www.lbhf.gov.uk/libraries
or by phone
0207 361 3610

h&f putting residents first

Hammersmith & Fulham Libraries

Write On...
RAINFORESTS

CONTENTS

Rainforests around the world

Tropical rainforests are warm, wet forests. They cover just six per cent of Earth's land surface, but they are home to around half the living things on the planet. Unfortunately, they are shrinking fast.

Tropical rainforests are found between the Tropic of Cancer and the Tropic of Capricorn (imaginary lines north and south of the Equator). Their climate is hot or warm all year round.

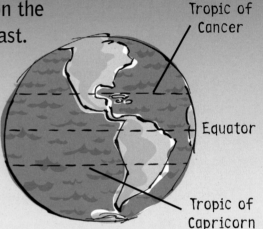

Tropic of
Cancer

Equator

Tropic of
Capricorn

Breathing forests

Rainforest trees and other plants produce a fifth of Earth's oxygen (the gas all animals need to stay alive). They give off the oxygen when they make their own food energy.

Not all rainforests are tropical. There are rainforests in cooler places, north or south of the tropics, such as the Pacific coast of North America.

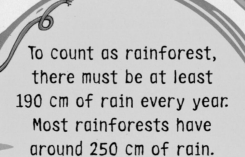

To count as rainforest, there must be at least 190 cm of rain every year. Most rainforests have around 250 cm of rain.

Mist rises from tropical rainforest on Borneo, in Southeast Asia.

Write On...

Try describing a rainforest from top (canopy) to bottom (forest floor). This will help you order your information – and make readers feel like they're really in amongst the trees.

High in the rainforest

At the top of the rainforest is a thick, green roof of leaves. This is the canopy. About two-thirds of the rainforest's plants and animals live here in the treetops. It's a busy, noisy place.

The canopy's leaves, flowers and fruit attract insects, birds and monkeys. Chattering and calling to each other, monkeys use all four limbs to swing at high speed between the trees – and some use their tails, too.

Beautiful birds

Flocks of colourful birds flit from branch to branch in search of food. There are parrots, birds-of-paradise, quetzals and toucans. Their eyecatching feathers and markings help them to attract a mate.

A few giant trees poke their heads above the canopy. They are called emergents. Some are as tall as twenty-storey buildings.

Birds of prey circle above the canopy. Harpy eagles keep their keen eyes peeled for a howler monkey meal.

Toucans live in many different habitats in South America, including the rainforest.

Write On...

Find out the names of different jewels to use as adjectives to describe the colourful feathers of rainforest birds. Try **emerald** (green), **sapphire** (blue), **ruby** (red) or **topaz** (orangey-yellow).

Monkey magic

Monkeys and their relatives are primates. There are primates in all the world's rainforests, except those in Australia. Primates feed on fruit, leaves and insects. They are perfectly adapted to live in the rainforest.

 Six kinds of ape live in rainforests: gorillas, chimps, orang-utans, bonobos, gibbons and ... people! Yes, humans are apes, too!

 Only New World monkeys have tails that can grip. They include squirrel, spider and capuchin monkeys.

 Lemurs are primitive primates. They live only on Madagascar, an island in the Indian Ocean.

 Howler monkeys are the noisiest primates. Their alarm calls can be heard 5 km away.

 Orang-utans have the longest arms (relative to body size) of any ape – three times as long as their body.

A spider monkey
hanging from its
tail and one arm in
the rainforest

Write On...

Use a thesaurus to hunt down interesting
verbs (doing words) for your writing.
Monkeys don't just move – they
swing, **loop**, **lurch**, **speed** and **sway**!

Piggyback plants

Millions of different plant species grow in the rainforest. It's dark and shady on the forest floor, but plants need sunlight. Many of them have come up with clever ways to receive enough light.

Lianas are vines. They put down roots into the ground, then climb up to the light by winding their thick, suckered stems around a tree trunk. The strangler fig grows in the opposite direction. Its seed sprouts high on a tree, then sends thick, long roots to the ground.

Living on air

Epiphytes are air plants – instead of having roots in the soil, they pick up moisture from the air. They live on the branches, trunks and leaves of trees. Bromeliads and orchids are epiphytes.

Orchids grow along tree branches. The biggest, the queen of orchids, grows a flower spike that's 3 m long!

Write On...

What would you **see**, **smell** and **hear** in a rainforest? Describe the **colours** and **perfumes** of the flowers and the **drip, drip, dripping** of the rain on the leaves.

Strangler figs' host trees eventually die and rot, leaving a fig 'tree' with a hollow middle.

Most strangler figs are supported by a tree – but not all. This one's roots are wrapped around a temple!

11

Understorey hunters

Beneath the crowded canopy is the damp, dark understorey. Dangerous predators lurk in this layer of the forest. They wait, motionless, for their prey. Brilliant camouflage helps them blend in with their surroundings.

The colouring of rainforest snakes makes them hard to spot — there are trunk-brown boas and leaf-green vine snakes. The chameleon is the king of camouflage among the reptiles. It changes skin colour to match its surroundings.

Camouflaged coats

Cats rely on camouflage, too. Stripes or spots blend in with the forest's dappled light. There are tigers, leopards and jaguars, as well as smaller cats. They hide on a branch, ready to pounce on passing prey.

The chameleon has another secret weapon besides its camouflage — a sticky tongue that shoots out at lightning speed to catch rainforest insects!

The green anaconda, which lives in the Amazon rainforest, is the world's largest snake. It kills prey by squeezing it to death.

A green tree python in the Australian rainforest

Write On...

Alliteration (repeating the same sound at the start of a word) makes your writing more interesting. Examples are **crowded canopy, damp, dark** or **pounce on passing prey.**

Amazing minibeasts

All sorts of minibeasts make their home in the rainforest, from hairy tarantulas to jewel-like beetles, and from marching army ants to fluttering butterflies. There are some insect record-breakers, too.

The world's largest beetle lives in the African rainforest. It's called the goliath beetle and weighs the same as a hamster. The world's longest insect is a stick insect from Borneo. Stick insects are champions of disguise. Many other minibeasts rely on camouflage to trick prey or hide from predators, but not all ...

Beautiful butterflies

Some insects are brightly coloured. Rainforest butterflies attract mates with their shimmering wings. Their bold colours warn predators that they are poisonous to eat.

Almost two hundred new species of insect are discovered in the Amazon rainforest every week!

Many different kinds of tarantula live in rainforests. The goliath birdeater tarantula is the world's biggest spider – it eats small birds and rodents.

The orchid mantis is disguised as an orchid flower. When insects come near for nectar, it snatches them and gobbles them up!

Write On...

Make up a poem about rainforest minibeasts. Think about their colours and how they move through the forest. Do they **flutter**, **scuttle** or **creep**?

The forest floor

It is gloomy on the forest floor, and the ground is carpeted with dead leaves. Worms, beetles and ants help the plant matter to decompose. Pigs, deer and larger animals move through the dappled shade.

 Army ants live in colonies of millions of insects. When they go on the march, they kill every insect and small animal in their path.

 Rafflesia, the world's largest flower, blooms in Indonesian rainforests. It smells of rotting meat.

 The tiny royal antelope lives in African rainforest. It is no bigger than a hare!

 The shy okapi looks like a cross between a zebra and a horse, but it's actually a cousin of the giraffe.

Africa's forest elephants eat a lot of fruit. They spread plants' seeds in their dung.

Write On...

An onomatopoeia (say *o-no-mat-o-pee-a*) is a word that sounds like its meaning. Think of examples that describe animals moving through the forest, such as **creak**, **rustle**, **slither**, **pitter patter**, **crash** and **thud**.

The okapi lives in the rainforests of Central Africa. Its main predator is the leopard.

Creatures of the night

Some rainforest animals sleep during the day and are busy at night. This back-to-front lifestyle is called being nocturnal. Special senses help these creatures to find their way and avoid danger.

Bats are active at night. They include the world's biggest bats, flying foxes. They use smell and sight to find nectar, pollen, flowers and fruit to eat. Smaller bats, such as vampire bats, use echolocation (a kind of sonar) instead.

Cute primates

Some primitive primates are nocturnal, too. Relative to their size, they have huge eyes and they locate their insect prey by sight. They include lorises and tiny tarsiers (a tarsier's head and body together measure less than 15 cm).

Sloths are nocturnal, but you probably wouldn't notice. Even when they are being active, they barely move!

Red-eyed tree frogs are active at night. Their shocking scarlet eyes help them to confuse predators.

A spectacled flying fox licks nectar from a flower in the Australian rainforest.

Write On...

Build up a treasure chest of wow words to describe the nocturnal landscape. Try **gloom**, **dead of night**, **darkened**, **midnight-black** and **secret**.

Rainforest rivers

Great rivers snake through some of the world's rainforests. They are a habitat for freshwater animals and plants, and forest animals visit them to drink. These waterways are also important transport routes.

The Amazon in South America is the world's second-longest river at around 6,400 km long. It is home to catfish, deadly piranhas, dwarf caimans (relatives of crocodiles), giant river turtles and two species of river dolphin.

Main waterways

Other important rainforest rivers include the Orinoco, also in South America, the Congo in Central Africa and the Mekong in Southeast Asia.

Giant water lilies bloom on the River Amazon. Their leaves are strong enough to support the weight of a toddler!

The basilisk lizard lives beside streams in the Amazon rainforest. It's light enough to walk on water.

Write On...

Stuck for a plot? Try setting a story on a small boat, heading upriver through the rainforest. What characters are onboard? And do they all survive the journey ...?

Rainforest peoples, such as these Betsimakara people on Madagascar, travel along rivers in canoes.

Rainforest peoples

People have lived in rainforests for thousands of years. For some, their way of life has hardly changed. The forest provides them with everything they need to survive.

Rainforest people gather fruits, nuts and medicinal plants from the forest. They hunt animals for meat and skins using spears, bows and arrows, slingshots and nets. As well as hunter-gathering, people plant food crops.

An uncertain future

People use wood, rattan and leaves from the forest to build homes and boats. Sadly, the destruction of the rainforests (see pages 26–27) is threatening rainforest peoples' traditional way of life.

On Papua New Guinea, it's traditional for Huli men to live apart from their wives and children. Men hunt and women farm.

The Yanomami of the Amazon rainforest hunt pig-like tapirs. They kill them with poison-tipped arrows. They get the poison from tiny tree frogs.

For special occasions, Huli men wear fantastic headdresses with feathers and flowers. They paint themselves with coloured clay.

Write On...

Write a speech about saving rainforest peoples' traditional way of life. What are the main arguments? Build them up, one by one.

Gifts from the rainforest

Many amazing materials, delicious foods and marvellous medicines come from rainforests. And with scientists finding new rainforest species every day, there must be many rainforest gifts left to discover!

 Many fruits and vegetables are originally from tropical rainforests, including mangoes, avocadoes, tomatoes and peppers.

 Cocoa and chocolate are made from cacao tree seeds. The ancient Maya drank hot chocolate spiced with chilli.

 More than two-thirds of the plants used to treat cancer are found in rainforests.

 The best gift from the rainforests is that they soak up carbon dioxide, a greenhouse gas, from our atmosphere. This helps to reduce the effects of global warming.

 Rubber trees come from Central and South America. The explorer Christopher Columbus brought the first rubber balls to Europe in 1496.

Write On...

Adjectives are describing words. Think of some words to describe mangoes or other rainforest fruits. Try **juicy**, **sweet**, **sticky**, **delicious** and **yummy**.

Mangoes and bananas from the African rainforest

Saving rainforests

Rainforests are disappearing. Already, more than half of the world's tropical rainforests have been destroyed, and an area the size of 80,000 football pitches is lost every day.

Rainforest is cleared for many different reasons. It is chopped down to make way for farms or mines. Some is cut for its timber (wood). Rainforest is also destroyed to make way for people's homes and cities.

What next?

Rainforests are so important. They are home to many unique animals and plants. That is why, around the world, people and organisations are fighting to save the remaining forests.

Teak and mahogany trees grow in rainforests. They are chopped down to make furniture and flooring.

When their habitat is cleared, rainforest animals are at risk of dying out.

HUNGRY HOMELESS
3 CHILDREN TO FEED

26

Kayapo people march to protest about a dam that will affect their rainforest home.

Write On...

Writing a news story? Think of a strong, snappy headline to draw readers in. Put across the most important facts in the first paragraph, called the standfirst.

Write On... Writing school

Are you ready to show off some of the terrific rainforest facts you've found out? First, decide on your form. Here are some ideas:

 A news story about a wonder-drug that's been discovered in the rainforest

 A short story about journeying up a rainforest river. What wildlife do you see? Do you meet any people?

 A blog – this could be by someone who has gone to live with rainforest people for a year

 If you like drawing, put across an important message through a comic strip, like the one below about palm oil:

A HUGE AREA OF RAINFOREST WAS CLEARED TO MAKE WAY FOR THIS PLANTATION OF OIL PALM TREES.

THE TREES PRODUCE PALM OIL, WHICH IS USED IN LOTS OF DIFFERENT EVERYDAY PRODUCTS.

BUT WHAT HAPPENS TO THE ANIMALS THAT ONCE LIVED IN THE RAINFOREST?

Write a letter or postcard to a friend. Pretend you are on a trip of a lifetime to the rainforest. Use the first person (I) to describe what you've been doing.

Hi Anil

Today I went looking for poison-dart frogs. They are called that because South American tribespeople use toxins from the frogs on the tips of their blow darts. The frogs are really colourful — orange, black and blue. This warns predators that they're dangerous to eat.

Lenny

Anil Patel
flat 203, Tall Towers,
Townsville, UK

Glossary

climate The average weather conditions of a particular place.

decompose Decay or rot.

echolocation Making a sound and sensing the echoes that bounce back to detect an object's location.

epiphyte A plant with roots that pick up moisture from the air. Bromeliads and orchids are epiphytes.

Equator An imaginary line around the middle of the Earth at an equal distance from the North and South Poles.

global warming The increase in the temperature of Earth's atmosphere.

greenhouse gas A gas in the Earth's atmosphere that traps heat. Carbon dioxide is a greenhouse gas.

habitat The place where an animal lives.

hunter-gathering Living by hunting wild animals and gathering wild plant foods.

medicinal Describes something that can be used as a medicine to treat illnesses.

New World The continents of North and South America.

nocturnal Active at night.

plantation A farm where one crop is grown on a very large scale.

predator An animal that hunts and eats other animals.

prey An animal that is hunted and eaten by other animals.

primitive An early form of something.

rattan A kind of palm tree with stems that are harvested and woven to make shelters or furniture.

species One particular type of living thing. Members of the same species look similar and can reproduce together in the wild.

toxin Poison.

tropical Having a hot climate.

Tropic of Cancer An imaginary line, north of the Equator. The climate in the area between this line and the Tropic of Capricorn is tropical.

Tropic of Capricorn An imaginary line, south of the Equator. The climate in the area between this line and the Tropic of Cancer is tropical.

Further reading and websites

READ MORE ABOUT RAINFORESTS:
Amazing Habitats: Tropical Rainforests by Tim Harris
(Franklin Watts, 2015)

The Big Countdown: 30 Million Different Insects in the Rainforest
by Paul Rockett (Franklin Watts, 2014)

Visual Explorers: Rainforests by Paul Calver and Toby Reynolds
(Franklin Watts, 2015)

READ MORE ABOUT BEING A GREAT WRITER:
How to Write a Story by Simon Cheshire (Bloomsbury, 2014)

How to Write Your Best Story Ever! by Christopher Edge
(Oxford University Press, 2015)

The Usborne Write Your Own Story Book (Usborne Publishing, 2011)

DISCOVER MORE ABOUT SAVING RAINFORESTS ONLINE:
kids.mongabay.com
A website with loads of information about rainforest animals.

www.rainforest-alliance.org
The Rainforest Alliance helps rainforest people to conserve their natural resources.
Its website has a great Kids' Corner.

www.rainforestconservation.org
The Rainforest Conservation Fund is another organisation that raises money to protect
the future of tropical rainforests.

Every effort has been made by the publisher to ensure that these websites contain no inappropriate or offensive material. However, because of the nature of the Internet, it is impossible to guarantee that the content of these sites will not be altered. We strongly advise that Internet access is supervised by a responsible adult.

Index

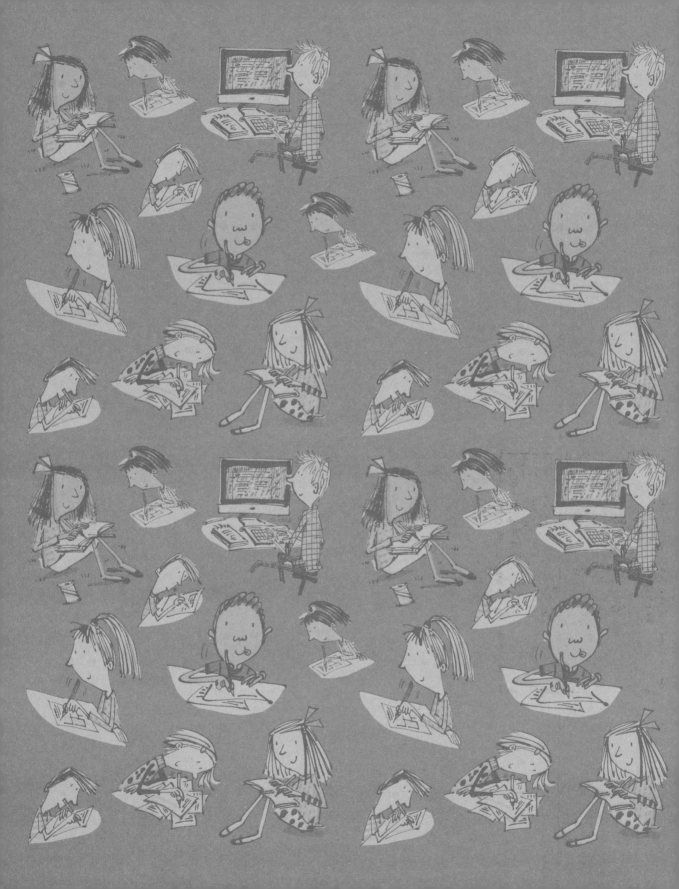